Plastic

Sally Morgan and Pauline Lalor

WHY WASTE IT?

SIMON & SCHUSTER
YOUNG BOOKS

WHY WASTE IT? has been researched and compiled by Simon & Schuster Young Books. We are very grateful for the support and guidance provided by our advisory panel of professional educationalists in the course of the production.

Advisory panel:
Colin Pidgeon, Headteacher
Wheatfields Junior School, St Albans
Deirdre Walker, Deputy headteacher
Wheatfields Junior School, St Albans
Judith Clarke, Headteacher
Grove Infants School, Harpenden

Commissioning editor: Daphne Butler
Book editor: Claire Llewellyn
Design: M&M Design Partnership
Photographs: Ecoscene except for page 29 Zefa.

First published in Great Britain in 1992 by Simon & Schuster Young Books

Simon & Schuster Young Books
Campus 400, Maylands Avenue
Hemel Hempstead, Herts HP2 7EZ

© 1992 Simon & Schuster Young Books

Printed and bound in Great Britain by BPCC Hazell Books, Paulton and Aylesbury

A catalogue record for this book is available from the British Library
ISBN 0 7500 1094 0

Contents

Plastic is very useful

Plastic is clean.   It can be bright and
colourful.   It is light but strong.
It will not rot or rust.

What things in your home are made of
plastic?

7

Plastic is made from oil

Oil is found deep under the earth. Wells are drilled to bring the oil up above the ground.

When it comes out of the ground, oil is black and very thick.   It is called crude oil.

Do you know any places in the world where oil is found?

Only part of the oil is used

Have you ever watched butter as it melts?
It separates into two parts – one part
is light and white, the other part is
heavier and yellow.   When oil is heated,
it separates in a similar way.

Crude oil is taken from the well
to an oil refinery.   There, the oil is
heated fiercely so that it separates.
The lightest oil is removed and is used
to make plastic.

11

12

Not all plastics are the same

Some plastics are hard.   They can be shaped to make things like tables and chairs.

Other plastics are soft.   They can be made into things like plastic bags or shower curtains.

What sort of plastics are in the picture?

Plastic keeps food clean

Plastic containers are used to store food, drink and other liquids. They keep dirt and smells out, and they are also very light to carry.

Think of all the things which are sold in plastic bottles. Why is plastic sometimes more useful than glass?

Plastic can be reused

You can wash plastic bottles and containers and use them again.

Some shops will refill your plastic containers if you take them back, rather than give you a new one.

Why do you think it is better to use a plastic lunchbox rather than plastic bags?

We throw away too much plastic

Many of the things we buy are wrapped in plastic or come in plastic containers.
It's a waste to throw these plastics away.
Some of them can be used to make new materials.   This is called recycling.

19

Plastic can be recycled

In a few towns, people can take their old plastic to a special collection point, called a plastics bank.

The different types of plastic must be put into separate bins.   They have to be recycled separately.

To make it easy to transport, the plastic is squashed into bales, and then taken to a factory for recycling.

New plastic from old

At the factory, old plastic is heated until it melts. Now it is ready to be made into new things.

Recycled plastic is not good enough to be used as containers for food or drink, but it can be made into many other things. Some are in the pictures. Can you think of any others?

23

Does plastic rot?

Some materials will rot if you throw them away.   They are biodegradable.

Most plastic never rots.   If it is thrown away outside, it will lie there until someone moves it.

Can you think of any other materials which are non-biodegradable?

More recycling, less rubbish!

The rubbish from our dustbins is collected each week and buried in huge holes in the countryside, called landfills.   Landfills are ugly, often smelly, places.   They attract animals which may spread germs.

Plastic rubbish takes up a lot of space. If we recycle more plastic, there will be fewer landfills spoiling the countryside.

Recycling saves oil

Oil is a very valuable substance.
We use it to make all sorts of things.
The fuel we use to drive our cars,
the tar we use to build roads,
the fabrics we use to make many of
our clothes are all made from oil.

Oil won't last for ever. One day it will
simply run out. We need to use it as
carefully as we can. Recycling plastic
is one way of saving it.

29

Index